FOR ALL THE CHANGIES DOING GOOD IN THE WORLD.

TABLE OF CONTENTS

THANK YOU!

JAN DHAENENS

MICHELLE PEDERSEN

LESLEIGH ROSS

JO DOYLE

TRUDDY CHEUNG

SINEAD HOUSTON

KIM CADIGAN

We found out that even comic books have lots of big and small words. Some work well together, while others don't and then there's the typos, grammar and spelling! A book like this simply doesn't happen without the help of many hands, heads and hearts and we'd like to thank our supporters all over the world for their encouragement, suggestions and inspiration.

A very special thank you goes out to our reviewers, who kindly gave up their time to read and comment on very rough drafts for six weeks and had to use their imagination as much as their sense of humour to make sense of all the craziness we came up with.

Thanks for being part of this adventure and for seeing the potential.

JESSICA MANTON

NARELLE MOORHOUSE

SAM McCUE

INTRODUCTION

I've never been a fan of traditional books - I've always been more of an audiobook person. With so many good change management books already out there, it had to be different and something even I would want to pick up and read.

I wanted to use the opportunity to create something that people could enjoy, learn a few things from it and not take too seriously. I've never tried drawing comics before so I really enjoyed having full creative licence to explore new concepts that just don't work in the strategic plans and documents I typically make for my clients.

This book is for leaders, managers and people who are not afraid to ask the hard questions and accept uncomfortable answers. I am super proud of what we've created together and it's just an amazing feeling to be able to share our creation with everyone who has a sense of humour and an interest in Change.

I hope this comic book and the tips inspire you to do your best work, that it makes you laugh and gets you through some of the rougher days. Go do good!

Peter Phan

I think my exact words were: "Nah, I really don't want to write a book" when Peter first suggested the idea of a comic in 2018.

Three months ago I drafted a list of 50 bad Change practices in 30 minutes on the train back home after a lunch with Peter and somehow that became 20,000+ words and hundreds of images. Good thing we had no idea how challenging the past two months would be, but we're still friends, even better friends maybe!

I hope we struck the right balance between poking fun at some of the ridiculousness in Change work and providing a way forward with the tips. You can read the five sections in whatever order you like, show it to your team and sponsor or gift the book as a subtle hint to your boss who needs a bit of help in the Change department.

Like with the Chameleon Cards in 2019, the goal of donating all the proceeds to charity (National Homeless Collective) inspired me to give it my all to make this the best book I could write. We've done our bit, now you go and make Good Change happen!

Gilbert Kruidenier

MEET THE BAD CHANGE TEAM

GILBURT THE CHANGE MANAGER
I AM JUST TRYING TO MAKE THE
BEST OF A BAD SITUATION!

CHUNTAO THE CHANGE AGENT
THERE'S NO SUCH THING AS BAD
CHANGE, AM I RIGHT?!

SAM THE SALESMAN
I CAN MAKE ANYTHING LOOK GOOD,
EVEN BAD CHANGE!

CHRISTINE THE CEO
I LOVE MAKING DECISIONS! GOOD ONES,
BAD ONES, I MAKE 'EM ALL!

IVAN THE I.T. MANAGER
PC BEING BAD? LET'S START BY
TURNING IT OFF AND ON AGAIN.

LINH THE LAWYER
COULD YOU PLEASE DEFINE 'BAD'
IN A LITTLE MORE DETAIL?

CLOE THE COMMUNICATIONS INTERN
BAD IS SUCH A NEGATIVE WORD,
LET'S GO WITH 'HAS POTENTIAL'!

FAISAL THE FINANCE OFFICER
CHANGE IS BAD FOR MY SPREADSHEET,
PLEASE MAKE IT STOP!

ELLIE THE ENGINEER
THERE'S NOT A BAD SITUATION THAT
MORE ENGINEERING CAN'T FIX!

PEDRO THE PROJECT MANAGER
KNOW WHAT CAUSES BAD CHANGE?
BAD PLANNING, THAT'S WHAT!

MANDY THE MANAGER
WHEN DID MICRO-MANAGING
BECOME A BAD THING?

QUINA THE QUALITY & SAFETY OFFICER
BAD PROCESSES MAKE FOR BAD
CHANGE, I ALWAYS SAY!

MAHA THE MARKETING MANAGER
EVEN BAD PUBLICITY IS GOOD
PUBLICITY, WIN-WIN!

ANDY THE ANALYST
WE ALL KNOW WHAT COMES OUT
IF YOU PUT BAD DATA IN...

HAJARA THE HR MANAGER
WE'RE NOT BAD PEOPLE BUT WE
DO SOME PRETTY BAD THINGS...

STEVE THE SPONSOR
THINK OF A BAD SPONSOR, MULTIPLY
THAT BY 4 AND YOU GET ME!

ROB THE RESISTOR
DO I GET TO SAY "I TOLD YOU SO"
WHEN BAD THINGS HAPPEN?

TINA THE TRAINER
I'M THE WORLD'S BEST TRAINER, WHY
IS EVERYONE SO BAD AT LEARNING?

UNO THE OFFICE UNICORN
THIS BOOK IS ALMOST AS
MAGICAL AS I AM!

LEADERSHIP

#1 Scope too big

#2 Rework due to continuous tweaks

#3 Allowing a sponsor to only pay lip-service

#4 Demanding results on impossible timeframes

#5 Not leading by example

#6 Lack of communication when it matters most

#7 Only focusing on the efficiencies

#8 Breaking promises

#9 Changing your mind every week

#10 The Power and Control approach

A DAY IN THE LIFE OF ROB THE RESISTOR...

ASSUMPTION

REALITY

LEADERSHIP #1
SCOPE TOO BIG
STARRING STEVE THE SPONSOR

TIPS ON STICKING TO YOUR SCOPE

Change projects and initiatives always start as an idea, unrestrained by timeframes, budgets and resource limitations. And that's how it should be because it allows us to imagine the best possible outcome.

Of course, there comes a time when you have to get real with your sponsor (Sorry, Steve!) and consider what you can actually accomplish with what's available and possible.

Here are some tips on how to set your scope and stick to it:

1. If you are a Change sponsor, resist adding new features (however cool/urgent) with every fibre of your being. A solid Change control process led by subject matter experts who review the impact of changes will be a big help to stay on time and within budget.

2. Spend a good chunk of your time on defining the various Change components. If you can, specify deliverables in detail and estimate how much effort it takes to achieve each one in hours. Do the math, see if it works in real life, adjust upwards if required.

3. Add 20-30% padding to your required resources because bad things will happen. If that's too much to ask for, don't start because it won't end well.

4. The person with the most subject matter expertise should decide the deadlines and budgets, not the most senior decision maker.

5. Keep reminding people that Change is not a mechanical process only, it takes time. Always has, always will and no amount of pressure will change that.

LEADERSHIP #2
REWORK DUE TO CONTINUOUS TWEAKS
STARRING CHRISTINE THE CEO

TIPS ON PREVENTING INFINITE TINKERING

It's the nature of change projects to create new circumstances and it's the nature of leadership teams to see opportunities. Put those two together and you can accomplish great things.

However, you can also end up in a situation where small tweaks keep being made to be 'just a bit more prepared' or 'just a little bit more aligned'. Better is the enemy of good and that's especially true for Change projects.

Here are some tips on what you can do to avoid tinkering after the plan is signed off:

1. Create a log of 'post-implementation improvements' and start a new project to get them done upon delivery of the initial signed-off Change.

2. Agree with the project manager that you will both stick to the plan and will not accept any new deliverable unless properly resourced and scoped.

3. Be firm with your leadership team or committee when additions are 'suggested'. They will respect you more for sticking to the plan than for failing to deliver on a promise you both knew you couldn't keep when you made it to please them.

4. Keep reminding the tinkering squad that their potential 5% improvement will take up a very certain 20% of the budget and add a month to the delivery date.

5. Make sure to address and update project metrics for time, budget and resourcing at every meeting. Paint a realistic picture and avoid baseless optimism.

LEADERSHIP #3
ALLOWING A SPONSOR TO ONLY PAY LIP-SERVICE
STARRING STEVE THE SPONSOR

TIPS ON SUPERCHARGING YOUR SPONSOR

The sponsor role is the most important role on the project, right after the end-user.

A well-selected sponsor can create a great project experience for everyone involved. When considering your options, keep in mind that enthusiasm and interest matter a lot more than seniority and organisational status.

Here are some tips on how to make the most of your sponsor:

1. Make sure they have at least 2-3 hours per week available for the duration of the project to support the change team and to meet them regularly for updates. Regularly means at least once every two weeks.

2. Choose a sponsor who is respected and not just liked. However, if they are both, that's always a nice bonus.

3. Provide them with a role description and KPIs that clearly explain what will be required, so they know what they are committing to from the start.

4. Offer them one-on-one coaching and upskilling in areas like project governance, delivery methods and the latest trends, tools and theories on Change management.

5. Keep them informed at all times and create opportunities for them to see the Change in action, have face-to-face interaction with impacted staff and users and promote the Change in different ways and places.

6. Never waste their time on trivial matters. Use them as a second-to-last resort when you've already tried everything else you could think of.

LEADERSHIP #4
DEMANDING RESULTS ON IMPOSSIBLE TIMEFRAMES
STARRING PEDRO THE PROJECT MANAGER

TIPS ON MANAGING TIMEFRAMES

The finer detail of Change work is not easily understood. Non-Change professionals who try to explain Change practices often end up waving their arms around, muttering words like people, values, empathy and then quickly try to change the topic.

Not a problem, that's why we're here! It's our job to meet stakeholders on their terms and speak their language, so we all know what can and what cannot be expected.

Here are some tips on managing timeframes:

1. However appealing, try to avoid building a reputation for being a 'superhero' who swoops in and saves the project. Turns out, there is always another project to save. What you're really doing by being 'helpful' is supporting poor planning and taking on responsibilities that are not yours to begin with.

2. Communicate upfront how long activities will take and present clear numbers for effort required and completion dates. If you have to adjust, have an explanation for each adjustment.

3. Check expectations at the start and Write.Them.Down! That way there is a single point of truth. They might change over time, but at least you'll have a record of how it all started.

4. It's a totally legitimate question to ask someone putting the pressure on to get things done how they would meet their own expectations if they were in your position. Their response will either give you an answer and a way forward or you will have learned something useful about them.

LEADERSHIP #5
NOT LEADING BY EXAMPLE
STARRING CHRISTINE THE CEO

TIPS ON LEADING BY EXAMPLE

If you are a leader of people, or even better a leader of Change, chances are your reports and others are watching you closely for the first signs of trouble with the Change.

You know how all those management classics tell you to walk the walk and talk the talk? Well, they are not wrong, because nothing kills commitment to change deader than a leader whose behaviour says: "Do what as I say, not as I do".

Here are some tips on how to lead by example:

1. Be aware of the optics and consider how decisions might be perceived. Even if the exec team hasn't had a raise in five years, perhaps it's not the best time to do so right after having announced a round of lay-offs or efficiency budget cuts.

2. In times of Change people need a leader, not a new friend. What they need from you is consistent guidance. Someone who shows vulnerability, is the first to try the new thing and who shares how the experience made them feel personally.

3. Acknowledge the effect the Change has on people and treat them as human beings not just resources. If you find this challenging, ask your Change person for some pointers, it's what they do best.

4. If people truly are your greatest asset, prove it by giving them what they ask for or find a better slogan. Decades of poor Change practices made people careful, and they will judge you by what you do more than by what you say.

5. Always speak the truth, especially when telling a lie is easier. People will appreciate an honest unpleasant message, delivered respectfully, a lot more than a lie that makes them feel good while keeping them in the dark.

LEADERSHIP #6
LACK OF COMMUNICATION WHEN IT MATTERS MOST
STARRING LINH THE LAWYER

TIPS ON AVOIDING GREEN STATUS DISEASE

Change can be very challenging to deal with. It's all good when it's smiles and high fives, but a lot less fun when it's anger and resistance every day. Don't pretend it's 'green lights across the board'. This is the time to 'keep it real'. Things will go wrong and there will be setbacks, it's a fact of Change.

Work to get a better story out there. Something that people can believe in, connect to and be informed by.

Here are some tips on how to communicate without giving people a bad case of 'Green Status Disease':

1. Keep it simple and say it like it is. Most Change narratives are not complex. We will do A to get to B by doing C, this is what good and bad look like and this is what we need you to do and how we will support you. That's it.

2. Staff trust their supervisor and CEO most, followed closely by their direct colleagues. Keep them informed, provide some talking points on the Change outcomes and why they matter and let them do the talking at any opportunity they get.

3. Get the word out there. If you ever needed a comms person, now is the time to get one and let them help you. If that takes too long for whatever reason, hire a copywriter and let them craft the story of the Change.

4. Keep repeating the same message to all stakeholders in different ways and settings because it takes a while for the message to land.

5. Answer any reasonable questions people might have about the Change with as much transparency as you can. If you don't supply the facts, people will happily make up their own!

LEADERSHIP #7
ONLY FOCUSING ON THE EFFICIENCIES
STARRING FAISAL THE FINANCE OFFICER

TIPS ON PUTTING PEOPLE BEFORE PROCESS

In our growth-focused and data-driven world a lot of work is still done by humans. And humans have emotions, thoughts and opinions that fuel important things like innovation, creativity and customer service.

You need both efficiency and empathy for successful Change. In most Change scenarios, you're better off focusing on the human effort behind the metric than plastering graphs and metrics all over the place. People, process, profit, in that order.

Here are some tips on how to put people before process:

1. While employees understand the need for profit, they will never care as much about the bottom line as you, so connect to their hopes and ambitions for the future instead and you'll have much more meaningful conversations.

2. Efficiency matters, but you need people to get it, so emotions matter more.

3. People prefer hearing the truth of the why, the business reasons behind the Change. It's a sign of respect and fairness if you just tell them how it is. They might not like it, but they'll respect you for your honesty.

4. Give people a chance to see the positives of the Change after they had time to process the negatives. Nothing is more annoying than someone continuously trying to sell you on the benefits while you're still processing the latest impacts on your colleagues and yourself.

5. If you have bad news to share, do it in person and have support options on standby. It's one of those spend-some-time-now-to-save-a-lot-of-time-fixing-issues-and-calming-things-down-later situations.

6. No one will remember all that stuff you said about savings, but they'll remember how you made them feel about the job they do every day.

LEADERSHIP #8
BREAKING PROMISES
STARRING HAJARA THE HR MANAGER

STAFF WERE PRETTY UPSET TO FIND OUT THEY WOULD LOSE THEIR JOBS – YOU PROMISED NO ONE WOULD GET FIRED.

I NEVER SAID THAT.

I WAS THERE – YOU LITERALLY SAID NO ONE WOULD LOSE THEIR JOB.

NOPE. WASN'T ME!

THERE'S A VIDEO OF YOU ON THE INTRANET SAYING THOSE EXACT WORDS.

THAT'S FAKE NEWS! DONT' BELIEVE EVERYTHING YOU SEE ON THE INTRANET.

TIPS ON PROMISES AND TRUST

Credibility of the messenger is everything when it comes to managing Change. Especially with high-impact Change, people will remember controversial and impactful statements for a long time. We also live in an age where everyone has a camera and isn't afraid to use it.

If you say something will happen in a certain way or at a certain time, people will take you at your word and hold you to it.

Here are some tips on how to make promises you can keep and build lasting trust:

1. Stay informed on the latest key developments and always remember the most important sentence in business: "I don't know, but I will find out".

2. Only promise things you know you can deliver. Sometimes that means telling people what they need to hear instead of what they'd like to hear.

3. If you can't deliver on a commitment, go back, admit it and negotiate a new deal. If you explain the situation and involve the stakeholders in the new deal, things can still work out.

4. Be as transparent as you can be and share good and bad news as it develops. Word always gets out, so be the first to spread it and have an opportunity to provide context. It's also a good idea to have back-up messaging ready to go, so you don't spend valuable time coming up with responses to new developments.

5. Tell the truth and let others speak their truth, even if you disagree with them. Inviting opposing views and opinions prevents groupthink and toxic cultures. Your project outcomes will be better for it!

TIPS ON MAKING DECISIONS THAT STICK

Every experienced leader will tell you that making big decisions is a lot harder than it seems. There are many perspectives, unforeseen consequences and real-world implications to consider.

In such uncertain times it can be very tempting to revisit decisions already made when new information presents itself. Change projects can get into trouble real quick when decisions are made based solely on ego, gut-feeling, short-term gains and past experiences.

Here are some tips on how to make decisions that stick:

1. Think and think again before you commit. Think through all the key components from different angles and make informed decisions based on data and subject matter expertise. Relying on intuition is very magical and inspiring, but there is no scientific evidence that it provides good counsel.

2. Doing things radically different in response to Change is hardly ever the answer in Change projects. All it does is create considerable delays and rework for the project team and show that the initial design was flawed to begin with.

3. Let the people most impacted by the Change have a say in decisions to be made, so you know you've included their views and opinions. Create a working group to gather input for your plan if possible.

4. Make decisions by consent so you can be sure that you've leveraged the smarts from all your best hires and experts and that they support the plan. Consent-based decision making speeds things up and helps with reflecting on what really matters.

5. Change takes time to emerge, stick with a chosen approach until you are absolutely sure it doesn't work. It's always a good idea to have a back-up plan, or two.

LEADERSHIP #10
THE POWER AND CONTROL APPROACH
STARRING MANDY THE MANAGER

TIPS ON PLAYING TO PEOPLE'S STRENGTHS

Despite their best intentions, micro-managing leaders can drive teams insane and out the door faster than anything else. If you hired smart people, why not let them do the job you hired them to do?

Sometimes you will truly know best, but unless you plan on doing everything yourself, allow your team some ownership and initiative and they will likely exceed even your own high expectations.

Here are some tips on how to get the most out of individual strengths of your team without resorting to micro-management:

1. You can't be an expert at everything, so acknowledge the skills and expertise of others as much as your own.

2. Avoid making one-sided decisions about tasks you don't perform yourself and negotiate boundaries about what your team can do with and without our permission.

3. Let your staff own the problem and help them find solutions instead of telling them what to do so they can prove that you can trust them to deliver good outcomes.

4. Engage a professional coach to find out why you feel the need to micromanage and let them help you to become a better version of your professional self.

5. Manage your team on outcomes instead of deliverables, after all, what works well for you might not work so well for them. Does it really matter how they get there if the work gets done on time and within budget?

READINESS

#1 Skipping the impact assessment

#2 Death by 1,000 slides

#3 Excluding difficult stakeholders

#4 Assuming resistance

#5 No time to get to know the new system

#6 Solo decision-making

7 Not hiring a comms person

#8 Denying your team issue ownership

#9 Over communicating

#10 Dismissing visualisation as 'unprofessional'

A DAY IN THE LIFE OF ROB THE RESISTOR...

ASSUMPTION

REALITY

READINESS #1
SKIPPING THE IMPACT ASSESSMENT
STARRING MANDY THE MANAGER

TIPS ON DOING AN IMPACT ASSESSMENT

The impact assessment is always featured in the top-5 of things you wished you had done earlier. It takes a lot of time to do well and freaks managers and leaders out every time.

You also need to ask so many hard questions that people can be forgiven for thinking that you're just there to make their lives miserable while you rip their beautiful strategy to very tiny pieces.

Here are some tips to make the most of the rare opportunity when you actually get to perform an impact assessment:

1. Make it relevant to the role and responsibility of the person/group you are talking to. Nothing freaks people out more than to get asked about things they have no clue about, so work within their context, after all, their lives are stressful enough as it is!

2. If you have enough time (at the start) get people involved and let them tell you the answers. The answer is almost always in the room. Someone knows a solution, you just have to find out who and get them to speak up.

3. If you have little to no time (which is most days...) prepare an assessment in draft and let people correct your preliminary scores.

4. When you present the assessment results, always present at least one solution for severe impact scenarios, so decision makers will have the option to adopt your solution or present a better one that works for them.

5. Always do an impact assessment, no matter how basic. Even if you can only spend 1-2 hours on it, it's your plan B for when things fall apart and can serve as a counter for over-optimistic desktop planning.

READINESS #2
DEATH BY 1,000 SLIDES
STARRING ANDY THE ANALYST

TIPS ON MAKING CHANGE LOOK GOOD

A big frustration for many Change managers is that people just don't seem to be interested in hearing about the plan until it's two days before the launch and then they want all the details. If you've been involved from the start or even only have written the plan based on a brief and a few meetings, you'll know more about the Change than 95% of the organisation!

What makes perfect sense to you, is most likely complete (and possibly unwelcome) news to everyone else.

Here are some tips on how to present your Change in an attractive and comprehensible way:

1. Five slides and ten minutes should be enough to explain the key components, leaving you with enough time to answer any questions people might have.

2. Design your presentation with all the detail in it and then stay high level in the first encounters with stakeholders. That way people can see that it's all there, but you're happy to just show them the highlights. You can always schedule a follow up meeting to go into more detail if required.

3. If your working with a team or division, brief their managers first so they can support you. That way they look good and 'in the know' and you'll have your first ally on board.

4. Keep it relevant to their context and involvement, try to find out what their major concerns are and address those before launching into detailed descriptions of how you see things. They won't hear a word you say until then anyway, so get that sorted first.

5. Keep in mind that you've been working on this Change for weeks or months, most others only just found out last week. Meet them where they are in understanding how this Change will work out and you'll have much more meaningful conversations.

TIPS ON HANDLING 'TOUGH CUSTOMERS'

We all dread the activist stakeholders who are in it for no one else but themselves and who are happy to get what they want at the expense of everyone else.

Despite all the corporate myths and urban legends, this doesn't happen very often and when it does, it's more often a case of lack of awareness of the needs of others than genuinely bad intentions.

Here are some tips on how to manage 'difficult' stakeholders in any Change project:

1. Always listen first; they might actually have a really good point. The Change might represent a real threat to whatever matters to them. Find out what drives their 'difficultness' and ask how they'd like to resolve the situation.

2. Point out that there's only so much in the budget and by giving them item A, B or C, you (they) are taking away something from team X, Y or Z. Make it personal and put a real-world consequence to their demands.

3. Enlist the help of your sponsor when things turn truly unpleasant, that's exactly what they do best.

4. Most of the time simply acknowledging a concern is enough to calm people down. You can listen to them without agreeing to anything and it doesn't cost you more than 10-15 minutes. That's a smart investment that will pay itself back many times over.

5. Stick to the plan as agreed and expect them to do the same. If it turns out the plan is bad that's not your responsibility. Don't choose sides or get caught up in political manoeuvering. Just do the job, deliver the Change and sidestep these situations whenever you can.

READINESS #4
ASSUMING RESISTANCE
STARRING ELLIE THE ENGINEER

HEY ELLIE, THAT'S A COOL COSTUME! WHERE'S THE PARTY?

NO PARTY. I'VE JUST INSTALLED A NEW AIR-CONDITIONER THAT USES 80% LESS ENERGY.

SO... WHAT'S THE PROBLEM? WHY ARE YOU DRESSED FOR WAR?

I'M EXPECTING A LOT OF RESISTANCE. PEOPLE HATE IT WHEN I TOUCH THE A/C!

WILL PEOPLE BE ABLE TO FEEL THE DIFFERENCE? HAVE YOU EXPLAINED TO THEM WHAT YOU'RE DOING?

NOPE. BUT I'M GOING WITH A 'STRIKE FIRST EXPLAIN LATER' POLICY!

TIPS ON INTERACTING WITH 'RESISTORS'

The commonly accepted narrative is that people resist Change and that's why it's necessary to manage resistance, nip it in the bud, mitigate it and meet it head on.

The reality of things is that people in general don't resist Change all that much, but they do get upset when they are kept in the dark until the last minute, misdirected or fobbed off with a half-baked plan. And can you blame them? How would you like it if that happened to you?

Here are some tips to avoid the pitfalls of resistance:

1. If resistance sounds like someone is stuck in a loop, it's likely they have genuine concerns about risks you might have underestimated. So, respond. And if you encounter an unexpected question, promise to get back to them and do so quickly.

2. Don't try to drag hard-nosed resistors across the line. Instead, focus on the vast majority willing to work with you. Some people will just never get on board, so invest the majority of your time and efforts in your early adopters, sponsors and influencers instead.

3. In most cases, resistance is a response to poor or absent communication. Get your Change story out there and keep repeating it until everyone has heard it at least a few times.

4. If resistance persists, review your plan to see if it's really as good as you think. Keep an open mind, it could be that in its current design the Change won't work and those pesky resistors are actually trying to warn or help you.

5. Give people some time to adjust. You've had weeks or even months to prepare and get used to the Change. You know exactly what is supposed to come next. They often only get a few days and one workshop to get on board - it's only logical they need a moment to make sense of it all.

READINESS #5
NO TIME TO GET TO KNOW THE NEW SYSTEM
STARRING TINA THE TRAINER

TIPS ON EASING PEOPLE INTO THINGS

A lot of Change is about introducing new systems and processes. Before the big roll out hits the 'end-user', hundreds of decisions have been made and months or even years of work have gone into it.

When it's four weeks before the launch and time for training, it turns out the world has changed and the new system and processes are no longer aligned with today's practice. And to make matters worse, that self-service user-manual that was part of the original support pack never actually got written... Yikes!

Here are some tips to get people to embrace the new approach instead of fighting it:

1. Lead with a comparison between the old and new, it's what everyone expects and does in their head anyway. This will show that you've thought things through and helps to catch some logic errors too.

2. Unless everyone is ready to get rid of the old and welcome the new, pay respect to the years of service the old thing put in. Legacy systems tend to develop personalities in people's heads and just like a real person will have good and bad sides. Acknowledging this, will make people feel like they are not being horrible, it's just time to move on.

3. Involve the end-user in the design. It's a cliché, but it still doesn't happen as often as it should and when it does, the wrong questions often get asked of the wrong people. If you believe this will just slows things down, you are probably right, but imagine how much rework is involved if you design a flawed and unfit-for-purpose system...

4. Ask for volunteers to be involved and don't just add it to their workload, give them enough time to be involved in a meaningful way. It's hard enough to do one job well, let alone dividing your time switching between the old and new ways of working!

5. Offer real-live scenarios and set up a sandbox (test environment) that users can play around in without some eager Project or Change manager hovering nearby. Instead provide some discrete feedback options to learn about their experience.

TIPS ON MAKING DECISIONS AS A TEAM

Hierarchies can be a really good thing. A little bit of structure to move things forward can be a big help. It's not so helpful if one person is making all the decisions and everyone else has to just do as they are told.

Even if you get the impression that people want you to make all the decisions, resist the temptation to give them what they want, because that's not what they need. Keep in mind, most days, people don't fight what they helped create.

Here are some tips on making decisions as a team:

1. If you want everyone to have a voice, give them time to think or you'll end up with the input of those two people who always have an opinion on everything. Send questions or an agenda ahead of the meeting to allow everyone to have a moment to think.

2. Be aware of group dynamics and keep an eye on the quiet ones. Don't take their silence for consent or even agreement. Offer multiple ways to provide feedback so you can draw on all smarts, not just the loudest ones.

3. Use a simple process like thumbs up-thumbs down voting, that works for the team or group and keep using it. After a while it just becomes part of how decisions are made. As long as everyone is in agreement that this is how decisions get made, it'll work just fine.

4. Address dominant and judgmental behaviours immediate by setting some ground rules and calling it out when people are breaking them.

5. Explain to managers and leaders that they can still have the final vote, as in, they get to speak last on a subject in a team session. If that's too challenging for them, you can offer to represent their views in the meeting and explain their absence, by saying to the team that their manager has consciously chosen to not influence the consultation and trusts their judgment to come up with a good solution.

TIPS ON SELLING THE BENEFITS OF COMMS

The number one complaint of most staff and one of the top-5 lessons learned from failed projects is that communication 'in this place' could be a lot better.

And yet, we're always so hesitant to hire a comms person because everyone knows how to communicate right?! Wrong, but it's one of those jobs that if done right, you hardly notice they are there.

Here are some tips on how to convince your sponsor to sign-off on hiring 'that comms person':

1. Use the argument that 'comms could be a lot better' and that this project needs a lot of it to succeed. Have a few examples on how you will use communication to engage, clarify and promote the Change using words, imagery and other media in a structured and consistent approach.

2. Most people have no idea what a comms person actually does. Make a very detailed practical list of all the things they will be doing in their role in support of the project. Don't just copy a role profile off the internet, write down the actual tasks. It's generally a list of 20-30 things that no one else is doing.

3. Present the hire as a key investment and highlight the positive impact on branding, engagement, promotion, understanding and presence. If leadership wants people to know about the Change, they'll have to provide you with an expert with words who can help make that happen.

4. Explain how comms is an actual job and everyone else on the project already has their own job to do, so who do they think is going to do that long list of things? It won't be you and it's not an activity to be done on the side.

5. Find examples of projects that worked really well for the organisation that had a comms person involved who made a real difference.

TIPS ON DELEGATING IN TIMES OF CHANGE

Not even micro-managers like being micro-managed and it's been topping the lists of 'things that make employees quit' for the past 30 years. Don't be that person.

Let your people do the things they are good at. You might be the best at everything, but there's only so many hours in a day and you don't want to spend all of them working while there's other people to do the job, right?

Here are some tips on how to keep delegating in times of Change:

1. Being trusted with relevant and important tasks gives people a sense of purpose and certainty in times of Change, it's the best thing you can do as a leader to inspire confidence and calm.

2. Take 15 minutes to provide a clear brief and answer any questions they might have, even the ones they think are silly. Assure them that they can ask more questions if needed, but leave finding solutions with them.

3. Don't just dump things on people because you're trying to 'empower' them. It will feel like they are being set up to fail. Be sure to discuss their level of capability and their workload capacity before handing over the task so you get what you need and they get to demonstrate their skills.

4. Keep an eye on progress but don't hover. Progress updates every few days is a reasonable expectation and also a good way to check their mental wellbeing and if they are on track.

5. If you are not sure if someone can do the job, give them the benefit of the doubt and make it 'safe to fail responsibly'. Agree on the level of support and involvement you will offer in advance and watch them go!

TIPS ON EARLY STAGE COMMUNICATION

We get it, we get it. You're super excited about the Change and want the whole world to know.

You've been carefully crafting your comms plan, key messages, newsletters and found the best images to tell the story. You even launched a SharePoint site and Teams channel with all the information and now people are telling you it's a bit much. What?!

Here are some tips to avoid flooding people with communication in the early stages of Change:

1. Start high-level and tell the story backwards (start with the predicted end/outcome). After that you can keep adding details over time to enrich the story and clarify the why of things as they happen.

2. Create a network of trusted communicators (direct managers) and give them speaking points for their team meetings, 1-on-1 and email updates so people hear it from a trusted source in a relevant setting.

3. Set up a simple comms plan that builds up the comms intensity across different media (newsletter, socials, SharePoint, notices, etc.) as the go-live date draws nearer. That way it will feel like a logical progression as they see the Change happen in front of their eyes.

4. Create a single point of truth where everything can be found, but still communicate across different channels to increase the reach of your message and use different levels of detail for higher impact and engagement.

5. Create a high-level roadmap that shows people where they are in the change at any point in time and explain how your message relates to that bigger picture.

READINESS #10
DISMISSING VISUALISATION AS 'UNPROFESSIONAL'
STARRING CHRISTINE THE CEO

TIPS ON WHY/HOW TO VISUALISE CHANGE

This book is perhaps the best proof that 'a picture is worth a thousand words'. All the same, we still spend heaps of time on crafting lengthy reports and massive slide decks in the hope that their sheer volume will convince leaders and staff that this is serious Change business.

Unfortunately, these works of art often get completely ignored and replaced by an off-the-cuff summary someone hastily read in an email instead.

Here are some tips to save your Change from this fate:

1. Change can be a hard concept to grasp, until you picture the old vs the new situation and all of a sudden you can have a conversation about what it looks like and how people feel about it.

2. Use images and stories to grab the attention and connect with audiences who are used to words and emails.

3. Use images and props to create a shared understanding of a concept, show the audience what you mean by collaboration, efficiency, new ways of working and discuss what they imagined it would be.

4. Videos, animations, interactive documents, simulations and/or games are an excellent way to get people to interact with the new reality of the Change, it allows them to experience it for themselves.

5. Logos, roadmaps and other relevant images can be very powerful tools to create a 'Change brand', something that helps people connect the dots between your Change and the information in front of them.

DELIVERY

#1 Rolling out the template and running away

#2 Sticking to targets when conditions change

#3 Insisting on using Change Model X

#4 Using made-up words to sound new and innovative

#5 Run a change just on KPIs and targets

#6 Disregard local differences

#7 Denying change fatigue exists

#8 Voluntelling people to be change agents

#9 Relying too heavily on technology

#10 Failing to learn from the final review

A DAY IN THE LIFE OF ROB THE RESISTOR...

ASSUMPTION

REALITY

TIPS ON SETTING UP FOR CHANGE SUCCESS

One of the most stressful (and exciting) times for a Change manager is when the time has come to put the plan into practice and start implementing.

You've spent weeks or maybe even months behind a desk, in meeting rooms and talking to people to get the lay of the land and now it's finally go-time!

Here are some tips to give yourself a running start and get set up for success:

1. It's a marathon, not a sprint. It sounds contradictory, we know, but burn-out is a real thing for Change managers and how does you working yourself into the ground in the first month help anything? Pace the Change and yourself and you'll still be around when all the pieces fall into place.

2. Go out and sit with the teams experiencing the Change if that's an option. Showing presence is the best way to show them that you're literally in it together and want to experience what they experience.

3. Schedule 2x the amount of time you think you'll need for a meeting so you never have to rush off. How you arrive and leave the meeting is what people remember and you want to be the first in and last out every time.

4. Prepare an FAQ with clear and concise answers to any possible question you can think of. Sometimes people would rather read it for themselves and have a think than talk to you in person. Provide that option and make some friends.

5. Create a space where anyone with an interest in the Change can meet an actual human to speak with, but also to see the plan, its goals, the available documents and most importantly a list of contacts in their area who can tell them more about the Change.

DELIVERY #2
STICKING TO TARGETS WHEN CONDITIONS CHANGE
STARRING STEVE THE SPONSOR

TIPS ON EVOLVING CHANGE METRICS

No practical Change plan survives its first day of implementation without modification. It's simply the nature of the profession and the things we do.

Not that this stops the more rigid and process driven project leads to try and hold on to those carefully crafted metrics, measures and indicators for dear life. Instead of displaying a long list of metrics that have little to do with your project.

Here are some tips on how to have metrics that make sense:

1. Co-design your metrics with the people in charge of what you are trying to measure. They are best suited to tell you how they know when things are going right and wrong.

2. Don't change the metrics too quickly. Building momentum takes time and slow doesn't equal wrong. Every time you change the metrics, your trending data starts from scratch, so it's best to really think them through in advance if you want to be able to show trending data six months from now.

3. Make the measurements relevant to the audience whenever possible. That's not as hard as it seems. Try something along the lines of: "This metric means A, it is related to your team because of its effect on B, which means that your outcome will be something like C".

4. Less is more. The less time spent on KPIs, the more you can spend on stakeholders. Of course it's impressive to have 50+ metrics to show you've got your eye on the ball, but what is even more impressive is if you have ten really good ones that actually tell the story of the Change.

5. Simulation is your friend. Create a mock-up dashboard if you can and 'walk' people through it. If they think it makes sense and have no burning questions at the end, you know you've got something to work with.

6. One minute per metric is a good guideline to hold to. If you can't explain the key message from the data in 1 minute or less, it's probably too complicated or not specific enough.

DELIVERY #3
INSISTING ON USING CHANGE MODEL X
STARRING ANDY THE ANALYST

TIPS ON CHOOSING A CHANGE MODEL

If you work long enough in any profession, you'll probably develop a special relationship with a specific tool, framework, method or model.

Nothing wrong with that, we get it. You've been through a lot together and have some really good stories to tell. That being said, applying the wrong model to a Change scenario can cause serious delays or even tank your project altogether. Fit-for-purpose is the key phrase here.

Here are some tips on how to choose a model that works for your Change:

1. All models are wrong, but some are useful. A model is mostly there to provide a frame of reference for everyone who is not you. It won't do anything but look pretty unless you apply it.

2. Simple is better. If you can do it in three phases or steps, don't go with 5, 7 or 8 steps (you know who you are…) just to make it look good. If you feel you can do without a step, take it out, but choose wisely and be sure to cover your bases.

3. Fall in love with the problem, not the solution. Some people with a love for hammers see nails everywhere. However, sometimes a screwdriver or drill is the better tool for the job. Equip your Change toolkit for solutions and don't just apply the same tool to every situation. It's not like you have limited options to choose from!

4. When in doubt, go with the classics. You can't go wrong with Kotter, ADKAR or Lean Change Management. Well, you can if you try hard enough, but it's easier to do change right than wrong with the classics and you can easily adapt them to your situation. They don't mind, they're classics for a reason.

5. Don't reinvent the wheel unless you absolutely have to. If the organisation has a preferred model they like to use and you can make it work, don't introduce something else! Count yourself lucky that they actually have a methodology in place and spare them the agony of having to adopt something for the sake of newness.

DELIVERY #4
USING MADE-UP WORDS TO SOUND INNOVATIVE
STARRING CLOE THE COMMUNICATIONS INTERN

TIPS ON SPEAKING PLAIN LANGUAGE

Change management initiatives don't have the best reputations. Sure, a large part of that is due to unrealistic expectations and unclear deliverables. The other part is people having to deal with grandiose, hollow and noisy proclamations that don't provide any real and useful information about the next Change. *Insert audible eye-roll*

It's gotten so bad with the flowery language that you'll positively stand out when you just say it like it is.

Here are some tips on speaking plain language when it's time to talk Change delivery:

1. If it's going to be a bumpy ride, you might as well own up to it and give people time to prepare. Of course they will be upset and respond emotionally, what do you expect? But this way, at least you get to pick when that happens.

2. Tailor the message to their level of involvement. Yes, it's easier to send a generic message, but you'll spend hours, if not days, to answer all the questions about the uncertainty that message creates. Individualised info sessions with the most impacted teams is your best and most time-efficient option here.

3. Listen twice as much as you speak so you don't miss any warning signs. It's common practice to try and (over)sell the Change on its benefits but when delivery time comes around, you'll get the most practical project feedback if you know how to listen.

4. A sign of true mastery is when you can explain something complicated in simple terms. People pick up on that and will trust you more readily than any use of big words and impressive graphs will ever accomplish.

5. Use examples and stories people are familiar with and ask trusted communicators to explain how things will work. This requires you spending time in operations to gather those stories and examples, but it's worth the investment and then some!

DELIVERY #5
RUN A CHANGE JUST ON KPIS AND TARGETS
STARRING PEDRO THE PROJECT MANAGER

Panel 1: SO I WAS THINKING WE SCRUM A BDD APPROACH AND ADD SOME MMFS LATER ON WHILE YOU TIMEBOX THE KPIS.

OH I THOUGHT WE'D USE BI AND ESM TO PIN THE KRAS AND SMEs TO ACHIEVE ROI.

Panel 2: NO CAN DO! WE NEED TO HIT TDD MARKERS IF WE WANT TO GET TO UAT BEFORE THAT.

SERIOUSLY? I THOUGHT WE'D WFH WITH THE POC TO GET THE NPS BY COB, IMO AT LEAST.

Panel 3: ARE YOU MESSING WITH ME RIGHT NOW?

OMG, I'VE NEVER BEEN MORE SERIOUS IN MY LIFE, SMH, LOL!

ACRONYMS:
SCRUM = Systematic Customer Resolution Unravelling Meeting
BDD = Behaviour Driven Development
MMF = Minimum Marketable Feature
KPI = Key Performance Indicators
BI = Business Intelligence
ESM = Enterprise Social Media
KRA = Key Result Area
SME = Subject Matter Expert
TDD = Test Driven Development
UAT = User Acceptance Test
WFH = Work From Home
POC = Point Of Contact
SMH = Shake My Head
OMG = Oh My Goodness
IMO = In My Opinion
LOL = Laughing Out Loud
NPS = Net Promoter Score
COB = Close Of Business

TIPS ON LOOKING BEYOND THE METRICS

All alphabet soup aside, it doesn't really matter how many acronyms you use to describe your performance indicator or what the project philosophy is, not everything in a Change project is about technology, metrics and milestones.

Only addressing the technical and measurable side of things like when launching an app, swapping operating systems or modifying a background process algorithm will just not work. Because…people!

Here are some tips on how to look beyond the tech, metrics and milestones and measure outcomes:

1. Measure what matters, not just what you have readily available. No one will contest that budgets, deadlines, training quota and deliverables are important in delivering Change. However, there are also staff satisfaction, user-experience, workload experience and solution adoption rates to consider, just to name a few.

2. Metrics matter, but people matter more, so divide your time wisely and use the metrics to engage in conversations, ask questions and design better solutions that lead to better outcomes for end-users or customers.

3. On time delivery is only part of the user experience. When people review the Change they just went through, they will also consider available information, support provided in every stage, responsiveness of the team, turnaround time on problem-solving and levels of engagement. Well, no one said Change work was easy…

4. The job is not quite done upon delivery. Meeting a deadline at the expense of people's physical and mental health is nothing to be proud of. Make sure support and resources are available throughout the change and that after-care is a fixed item in the plan. It's an easy way to create positive publicity at the water-cooler.

DELIVERY #6
DISREGARD LOCAL DIFFERENCES
STARRING FAISAL THE FINANCE OFFICER

TIPS ON USING LOCAL EXPERTISE

The times of taking a generic approach to Change are over, even if some leaders still didn't get that memo.

No more steamrolling the same Change method across teams and divisions, regardless of their differences. Change practices have improved significantly over time. Nothing is more frustrating for people than having to perform actions that have no relevance for their local circumstances only because "the template says so".

Here are some tips to use local expertise to make the most of Change in every setting:

1. One-size fits most, but not all, so try to be flexible when it comes to applying the same rules and expectations to teams that will be heavily impacted versus teams that are only marginally affected.

2. Different teams can be in different stages of the Change and will need time to get organised. Until they do, you will not get through to them with all your plans, ideas, tasks and requirements. Meet them where they are and work from there, while showing them the path forward and the tasks ahead.

3. There are many ways to get the same outcome. Let the team worry about the how as long as they align with the why and the principles of the Change. People hardly ever fight what they helped create, so why not make it easy for everyone?

4. Good practice is better than best practice because that best practice worked in exactly one setting and it's probably not yours. Get local teams to explain to you how the Change might be adapted to suit the local circumstances best.

5. Never underestimate cultural differences between teams, new acquisitions or even different parts of the same organisation. See if you can get a good mix of people to work together on what might be the best way to introduce the Change so they can see that they are really quite similar when it comes to getting things done.

DELIVERY #7
DENYING CHANGE FATIGUE EXISTS
STARRING MANDY THE MANAGER

TIPS ON DEALING WITH CHANGE FATIGUE

Even amongst Change professionals there is no unanimous agreement on whether Change fatigue is a real thing or not.

Some argue that it's just resistance by another name, others say that it's absolutely real and one of the main causes of people burning out on the job.

It's one of those situations where it's better to be safe than sorry.

Here are some tips on how to best deal with Change fatigue:

1. If people tell you they are tired of Change, acknowledge their experience and let them tell you why. Ask what could help them deal with the next Change and what their solutions might be. You don't have to agree with them, just listen and they'll feel a lot better for speaking up.

2. Work with the project manager and executive team to always have a current overview of how much Change is going on at any time and agree on a maximum level of Change activity at the same time.

3. Share the overview of the main current and upcoming Change projects with all employees so everyone can see what's going on. It'll provide some much needed perspective and also help with priority setting.

4. Resist the temptation to add just one more Change. Set a limit and stick to it, we all know that pouring more water in an already full glass gets real messy real quick.

5. Make sure your trusted and preferred 'senders' keep communicating the path forward if there's no other option than to keep going ahead with the Change and remember to invite as many stories of people's personal experiences as possible to 'give a face' to the Change.

DELIVERY #8
VOLUNTELLING PEOPLE TO BE CHANGE AGENTS
STARRING CHRISTINE THE CEO

TIPS ON CREATING A CHANGE AGENT TEAM

Change agents, champions, supporters or whatever name you want to give them, can be an invaluable asset to your Change initiative.

As a formal part of the Change team they'll be your eyes and ears who are best positioned to spread the word, provide additional detail and answer the basic questions their teams and colleagues might have.

Here are some tips on how to create and make the most of a team of Change agents:

1. Ask for volunteers (often your early adopters, but not always) and provide a clear brief that includes an estimate of time per week required.

2. Explain their role as 'eyes and ears' to the rest of the organisation. They are there to listen and pass on issues, not solve everyone's problems or listen to complaints all day.

3. Make them clearly identifiable through props like water bottles, t-shirts, lanyards, digital backgrounds, special avatars or anything else you can think of that makes them identifiable as a Change agent.

4. Arrange regular meetings where they hear the latest developments first and get a chance to share observations and ideas from the frontline.

5. They already have a job and are doing this to support the organisation, so get their managers to commit a few hours per week for the agents to support the Change in different ways.

6. Give them recognition and exposure on a regular basis, even if they were voluntold. The currency in Change is information and recognition and you can provide both for free.

7. Let them speak about the Change in their own way, with or without using (enterprise) social networks. They don't have to be cheerleaders, as long as they present facts and not opinions.

DELIVERY #9
RELYING TOO HEAVILY ON TECHNOLOGY
STARRING IVAN THE I.T. MANAGER

TIPS ON USING TECH TO SUPPORT CHANGE

Technology can be your friend in Change projects. Or your worst enemy. Done right, technological solutions can be a great benefit to changing circumstances. Done wrong, you can cause a lot of stress and anxiety.

Most people would not want to go back to a world without the internet or flushing toilets and while we personally can't think of a downside to flushing toilets, we also know that the internet has its dark sides too.

Here are some tips on how to use technology to the advantage of your Change:

1. Faster isn't always better. An unfamiliar system that moves quickly can easily cause people to feel like they can't keep up. If you highlight the similarities and compare new versus old operations, they'll soon see how the technology actually supports them in meaningful ways.

2. Getting used to new tech while learning new processes and ways of working can make people feel incompetent and uncertain about tasks they used to master. Provide enough time for training and getting used to the system and train a group of super-users to answer questions and show how it's done.

3. The threat of 'the robots taking over' is very real for some people. Your best option is to demonstrate how automation of boring, repetitive tasks creates time to focus on value-adding tasks that they enjoy more and that computers just can't do.

4. Create a one-page overview that maps which technology, apps and platforms will be used for each part of the change and provide easy-to-use support through a service desk, additional training and FAQs. Most people will be able to self-help if you provide accessible support systems. Capture and share their user-stories too!

5. Make sure you have users involved asap from the start in getting the requirements, testing and system design. The technology is supposed to be designed to serve the end user. It's a nice bonus that you can inspire people with stories from their peers who were involved from the start.

6. Address the 'fear of the new'. Acknowledge it as a natural part of the change process and nothing to be embarrassed about. Give people a platform to share their experiences with the new technology and processes so others can adopt their mindset and lessons learned.

DELIVERY #10
FAILING TO LEARN FROM THE FINAL REVIEW
STARRING THE PROJECT CONTROL BOARD

TIPS ON RUNNING A FINAL REVIEW

The final review is low on the list of favourite things for Change professionals. It's like herding bored or busy cats and everyone just wants to move on.

All the same, it is also the time where you can record lessons learned and opportunities for improvement.

Another important feature is that marking a distinct point of 'done', gives people a sense of completion and that it's okay to now move on to other things.

Here are some tips on how to run an effective final review:

1. Make the final review a fixed part of the planning process and schedule enough time to do a proper job. 2-4 hours doesn't seem too much to ask after you've just spent 12-18 months on delivering the Change, does it?

2. Find a template that helps to spend an equal amount of time on every phase of the Change so you don't end up with some scattered notes about only the very last part that people remember. Maybe try the 4L-retrospective to keep thing structured (just Google it).

3. Invite as many perspectives as possible to get a true sense of what worked and what didn't. The added bonus is that people will appreciate the opportunity to be heard and share their point of view one last time.

4. Change only happens when people can see the difference. Not all changes made will be obvious, so by publishing the lessons learned, everyone gets to see the difference and will benefit from the experience.

5. This is not the time for evening scores and assigning blame. Use that time more productively to find root causes for issues that emerged and explanations for things that didn't work. Don't make or take this personal, if a Change initiative fails completely it's hardly ever because one person made a mistake.

COMMUNICATION

#1 Sending emails to avoid human contact

#2 Chickening out of bad news

#3 Denying the change team access

#4 Q&A without any A's

#5 Innovatifying everything!

#6 Data dashboard overload

#7 Leaving the comms to the last minute

#8 Never-ending stand-ups

#9 Sugar-coating change consequences

#10 Shouting to get the message across!!

A DAY IN THE LIFE OF ROB THE RESISTOR...

ASSUMPTION

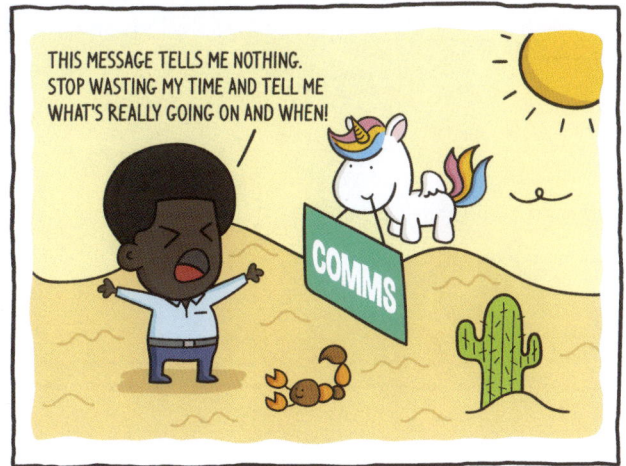

REALITY

COMMUNICATION #1
SENDING EMAILS TO AVOID HUMAN CONTACT
STARRING STEVE THE SPONSOR

TIPS ON HUMAN DYNAMICS

The most difficult part of Change is the human side of it.

There are so many different responses and emotions you can encounter that the possibility of being misunderstood or misinterpreted seems a certainty.

The only certainty in Change is that hiding in an office far away from the action and writing wordy plans and emails is not the answer.

1. Here are some tips on how to connect with the human side of Change:

2. Meet them where they are in the Change process. This is often quite different from where you are or even where you want them to be for things to move along at pace. Start slow, finish fast(er).

3. Logic doesn't work on fear (Fake Evidence Appearing Real) of any kind. Fear eats logic for breakfast so stop feeding it. Explore the fears that are present and work through them by listening and supplying facts to replace assumptions and rumours. You'll find that logic takes over after the fears have been addressed properly.

4. Create a safe port in the Change storm by communicating what stays the same despite the Change. This could be colleagues, clients, a workplace, systems or even a key part of the process that doesn't need changing.

5. Let people tell their story even if you have to listen to it a few times. What you're hearing is them making sense of the Change in real-time, no need to even say anything, just listen.

6. Create distinct moments of transition from the old to the new using rituals or ceremonies. This could be a tongue-in-cheek sendoff of the old system/process, a launch party morning tea, a milestone celebratory round of coffees or a BYO lunch session where people share their Change experiences. People will stop to take a breath when they know the job is done, so provide a clear signal and reflect on how far you've come already.

TIPS ON BREAKING BAD NEWS

Sometimes Change is just bad news. Like losing colleagues to budget cuts, long-held privileges slowly disappearing, your team moving floors (and you had the best spot ever!) or even worse, losing your job.

Delivering bad news is a skill in itself and a task that requires preparation and empathy.

Here are some tips on how to break bad news the right way:

1. Schedule a meeting with a clear topic and agenda and view it as the first part of a conversation. There is likely to be some shock or anger and you don't want people to respond when they are not the best version of themselves. Make yourself available for at least one more follow up meeting to answer questions.

2. Consider the most likely scenarios and have answers for the most common questions people could ask. That preparation will give them clarity and comfort. It will also show that you're taking this very seriously and are doing the best you can to support them.

3. It's all in the delivery. Lead with the bad news, straight up and without sugar coating. Be respectful and give them some time to let it sink in. Sit in silence and give space to the emotions they experience. Then discuss next steps. A good question to ask is: What would you like to do next? If they need time to think, give them as much time as you can afford.

4. When you manage to respect people's dignity and humanity, it's quite common that they will thank you for your honesty and respectful approach. You'll still feel horrible, though, that's just the way it is with bad news.

5. However horrible you feel, never make vague promises that you can't keep. It's downright cruel to give people false hope just to make them or yourself feel better.

6. If you think a person will become extremely upset or aggressive, never have the conversation alone. Invite one more person to the conversation and explain their presence in advance as being an objective observer to ensure everyone gets treated fairly.

COMMUNICATION #3
BLOCKING ACCESS TO INFORMATION
STARRING LINH THE LAWYER

TIPS ON KEEPING TEAMS INFORMED

Perhaps one of the biggest frustrations of Change Communications is that you can engage, clarify and promote for months and still people will only engage with the Change two weeks before everything needs to happen!

A close second are (most often) managers who keep things from their teams to 'protect' them. Seriously, we're all professionals and grown-ups here, no need for that.

Here are some tips on how to keep teams informed at all times:

1. Provide a place for interested people where they can find reliable information. Perhaps a room, shared area, an office wall, SharePoint site, website, intranet page or MS Teams space just to name a few.

2. Start early and provide regular (at least weekly) updates to show progress and keep them interested.

3. Share the same information across different channels, like team meetings, notice boards, the intranet, social media accounts, communal areas and yes, even the back of bathroom doors is excellent real estate to reach a captivated audience.

4. Find your company's 'influencers' and ask for their help in spreading the word of new developments. You can give them some key messages and talking points and then leave the rest to them. Influencers like being the first to know and spreading the word, so use that to your advantage.

5. Provide different levels of detail for different levels of involvement. Think of it like social media updates. A Pin or Tweet format for a quick update on something specific, a Facebook post-like message with pictures for a story or a LinkedIn update to share some professional lessons learned. Get creative and get noticed.

6. Check if information is getting 'out there' by simply walking around (or the online equivalent) and asking if people have heard about so-and-so already. If they have, great, if they haven't that's a good opportunity to tell them and give them more time to prepare.

COMMUNICATION #4
Q&A WITHOUT ANY A'S
STARRING ELLIE THE ENGINEER

Panel 1:
HEY EVERYONE! THANKS FOR COMING TODAY TO DISCUSS THE UPCOMING CHANGE.

THE TEAM HAS BEEN LOOKING FORWARD TO THIS. FINALLY SOME ANSWERS ON THIS CHANGE!

Panel 2:
HERE'S A DOCUMENT WITH SOME QUESTIONS AND ANSWERS MANAGEMENT PREPARED EARLIER.

PERFECT! EXACTLY WHAT WE NEED.

Q&A

Panel 3:
UM... WHY ARE THERE ONLY QUESTIONS AND NO ANSWERS?

YEAH ABOUT THAT... MANAGEMENT ASKED US TO CO-DESIGN THE ANSWERS WITH YOU AND THE TEAM...

1-PAGE CHANGE PLAN

TOOLS

TIPS ON HELPFUL Q&A DOCUMENTS

In an ideal world, each Change initiative is co-designed and engineered with the help and early involvement of key stakeholders.

But we don't live in an ideal world - sometimes the first time you get to actually see them is at the Q&A session that should answer all their questions...

Here are some tips to make the most of Q&A sessions and documents:

1. Try to pre-empt as many basic questions as you can, so people can see you've thought this through. Think of things like timeframes, people involved, next steps, budgets, event sequences, reasons for decisions and be as transparent as possible.

2. It's not uncommon for a Q&A document to get very detailed and contain more than 100 items. It could get messy quickly. Arrange information in sections, topics, impact and/or stages, whatever makes sense for the Change initiative and the people involved. Extra points if you can make it searchable and sortable online!

3. Provide a 'human option' for people who prefer to speak to a person about their personal circumstances that the Q&A doesn't cover. Try to get the Change Sponsor involved as much as possible too.

4. Update and publish the Q&As in an easily accessible place and format (paper and digital) so everyone has access to the same information. It doesn't matter if they use it or go there, it matters that it's out there.

5. In face-to-face sessions, listen to the asked and unasked questions, then answer both. You want maximum clarity about what will happen and the intent of the Change activities.

6. "I don't know, but I will find out and let you know" is your biggest friend when you don't know the answer. Share the outcome publicly to show there are no hidden agendas or secret plans, it was a good and unexpected question that provided an opportunity to create more clarity, thanks!

TIPS ON HOW TO BE TRULY INNOVATIVE

Being innovative is like being famous, if you have to constantly tell people how famous you are, you're probably not that famous…

The simplest definition we know for being innovative is 'doing things new to you and your customers'.

Innovation and creativity are closely related and instead of starting out by saying: "Oh, I am not creative at all!", give it a go and create the conditions that bring out your inner innovator.

Here are some tips on how to adopt an innovator mindset:

1. Despite popular belief, stress and looming deadlines are not great for creative thinking. Create some space and time to sit with an idea and look at it from all angles. Give it time to grow.

2. Draw it, write it down or create a presentation to help share the idea with others and don't worry if it doesn't look polished. If it's a good idea, people will get it and they are more likely to add to a work in progress than to something that looks like a perfect prototype.

3. Run (controlled) experiments to bring the concept into the real world to see what it does. Call it beta-testing, sampling, piloting or a simulation, as long as you get it out of your head and 'out there' for others to interact with the idea.

4. A small change to an existing concept that makes it fit the context of your organisation is more valuable than a totally new method or process for people to learn while already busy.

5. Say: "yes, and…" to suggestions instead of "…no, I want…". We know that making co-creation work is much harder than it seems, and we also know it's totally worth it because even only two minds already know more than one, however experienced and brilliant.

6. Get comfortable with failure, because innovation requires some risk taking and doing things differently. It won't always end well, but you'll learn something new every time!

COMMUNICATION #6
DATA DASHBOARD OVERLOAD
STARRING ANDY THE ANALYST & ELLIE THE ENGINEER

TIPS ON BUILDING EFFECTIVE DASHBOARDS

With all the talk about Artificial Intelligence, Big Data and data mining you'd expect to be able to get an update on where things stand with the Change at the push of a button.

This is unfortunately not the experience of most Project and Change managers. The exact opposite is true more often than not and even if the data is there, it's presented poorly and mostly irrelevant to stakeholder.

Here are some tips on how to set up dashboard that help show the Change in progress:

1. Let teams and leaders create their own dashboard, you'll find that most teams end up with similar metrics, but the difference is that they, and not you, chose those metrics.

2. If you have the data and technology, allow drilling-down, downloads and customisation so that teams can see and analyse what matters most to them and react accordingly.

3. Like in a car, a dashboard is not a report or a manual, so only present the truly essential details. Maintaining a very detailed dashboard every week is very expensive and too many dials and numbers will confuse the decision makers and have them run off the road.

4. Display the data in communal spaces where people can interact with the progress being made and use a variety of formats that makes metrics uniquely recognisable and part of the brand of the Change.

5. Risk adversity and the misconception that your organisational data or project needs are unique can lead to very costly 'in-house development' of secure dashboards and reporting. There are excellent applications on the market that come with monthly security upgrades and maintenance at a fraction of the cost and time of a corporate do-it-yourself build.

TIPS ON BEING CONSISTENT AND TIMELY

Just because you said it or sent an email doesn't mean people actually heard, read or understood it, even if they joined the meeting.

It can be very frustrating to feel like you've been repeating yourself over and over and you're just not getting through.

The good news is that you are getting through. The bad news is that it takes planning, consideration of different viewpoints and patience for the message to sink in.

Here are some tips to get your message heard and understood:

1. Involve your comms person at the very start and let them do the communication work for you. Edit their drafts if you have to, but take their advice on timing and content to heart. Trust that they know what they're doing even if your style is different.

2. Have a plan for scheduled communications and stick to it no matter what. After just a few messages your stakeholders will start looking for the next update on its regular day and that's when you know it's working.

3. Start weeks in advance of the Big Change Day if you want to have an authentic two-way conversation instead of simply broadcasting what will happen next.

4. Tell a big story in smaller parts. Start with the big picture and then zoom in on the steps in between through weekly updates in team meetings, stand-ups and emails.

5. Use the same kind of language and terminology every time. This creates a common language and understanding before the Change happens. By the time it comes around people will know the right words and key topics back to front.

TIPS ON MAKING THE MOST OF STAND-UPS

Stand-up meetings are a very effective way to share a lot of information in a short time and keep everyone on the same page for the day working towards the same goal.

15 minutes in the morning is generally enough for everyone to quickly share what they've finished, what they are working on and what is coming up. Bigger in-depth discussions are taken offline and reported on the next day, while everybody else goes back to work on their own tasks.

Here are some tips to make the most of stand-up meetings:

1. Use the opportunity to make it a team event by opening with a few short announcements like birthdays, life events and special recognition or whatever is relevant for the whole team to hear. If it involves cake, even better!

2. Have a fixed format that everyone is used to and knows how to use. Whether you use a board, props or just a spoken update, as long as everyone answers the same questions the meeting should move forward quickly.

3. Run a countdown timer that tells everyone exactly how much time there is left and have a process in place for politely interrupting if someone is going into too much detail.

4. Have the meeting out in the open and welcome visitors who just want to listen in. If they have questions they can ask them, but the answer might be taken on notice and reported back in the next meeting.

5. Share decisions and progress for everyone to see on an office wall or in an accessible digital space where people can go and see the status of an issue or topic for themselves.

COMMUNICATION #9
SUGAR-COATING CHANGE CONSEQUENCES
STARRING CHRISTINE THE CEO

TIPS ON CRAFTING KEY MESSAGES

Think of key messages as the 30-second summary of the Change, the main things you want everyone to know about the upcoming events and what it might mean for them.

Key messages sometimes get confused with speaking points. An easy way to tell the difference is that speaking points will vary for each phase of the project, while key messages basically remain the same from start to finish.

Here are some tips on crafting informative key messages:

1. Challenge yourself to set a limit of 5-8 key messages. That might sound reductive, but the Change project will run for months and more details can always be shared later. Your first priorities are clarity and focus.

2. If your messages address the project's 5W and 1H (what, why, when, who, where and how) in every communication, you're significantly increasing your Change's chances of success.

3. Start at the highest level (organisation) and then adjust for the major key stakeholder groups if you can. That doesn't mean you rewrite them, just change a few words here and there to make it more fitting to their context.

4. Don't try to sell the Change with overly positive language and niceties, it will only damage your credibility, let people make up their own minds free of (well-intended) manipulation.

5. Test the messages on known sceptics and critics in confidence before you start communicating to a broader audience. If they find them informative and useful, others will probably think the same.

6. You'll be repeating these statements more than a few times, so make sure you are comfortable with the content and style. You don't want to feel like you continuously need to adjust and rephrase them.

7. Feel free to use metaphors or references to known situations to clarify the intent and goals of the Change, as long as they support understanding and don't become so complicated that people lose the plot.

TIPS ON USING DIFFERENT MEDIA

Communication, or more precisely the lack of communication is the cause of most issues in Change projects.

That's because most people consider communication to be just spoken or written words. Turning up the volume or spamming people's emails will simply not work.

Applying a narrow definition of communication robs you of a lot of possibilities and opportunities for meaningful engagement.

Here are some tips on using different media to get the Change message across:

1. Not all people absorb information in the same way, so for Change communication it's not either…or.. it's and…and…Use a mix of words, imagery, sound, visuals and tactile experiences to share your message.

2. If you can get the budget, time and space, set up an experience or simulation environment with that new system, office environment, workshop set up or new process to let people interact with it in real life. Remember to record their feedback on the experience so you can improve on the final design.

3. Visualise the Change through artefacts in the workplace, like signs saying "this is where the new creative space will be", or wall-sized posters showing the benefits of the new situation in images of the future state.

4. Create short live-events of 15-30 minutes with key figures of the Change who can do a broadcast, live Q&A or BYO lunch meeting to answer questions or have debates on good practices for the Change.

5. Set some professional guidelines and use video apps to let teams and individuals share with the rest of the organisation what the Change means to them and how they plan to deal with the necessary changes.

STRATEGY

#1 Doing what the competition does

#2 Initiating unnecessary change

#3 Investing in useless training

#4 Squeezing for efficiencies

#5 Hiring consultants for everything

#6 Not budgeting for change

#7 Long term goals with a short-term mindset

#8 Fixating on 'the culture'

#9 Worst.Project.Name.Ever

#10 Running change like a military drill

A DAY IN THE LIFE OF ROB THE RESISTOR...

ASSUMPTION

REALITY

TIPS ON GOOD VS BEST PRACTICES

Best practice is one of those stale and overused phrases. It holds the promise of a shortcut to success, an easier way to accomplish a difficult task and a certain way to the top.

In reality, best practice is a high-level summary of an organisation's long road of discovery that involved many moving parts. It's highly unlikely that you (or they for that matter) would ever be able to replicate their process and get the same result. Not that this has ever stopped businesses from trying!

Here are some tips on good instead of best practices:

1. Good practice starts with good process. Review your key processes for task clarity and effectiveness with the people in the process. Maybe all that is needed for a big improvement are a few small and easy adjustments and some different words.

2. Your Change strategy of choice should fit the challenge and your organisation's culture and capabilities. At one point everyone wanted to be like Google, until even Google became something else. Choose your idols carefully.

3. Before you commit, do your research and collect evidence that proves that this best practice is indeed the best option. You wouldn't want to change your whole business model based on some anecdotal evidence and a few 'expert' opinions, now would you?

4. Set realistic timeframes (5-10 years) based on a detailed plan of how to get from where you are now to how you will rival the best in your field while they continue to evolve. That plan will tell you how likely success really is and what it will cost you to achieve that last 5% difference between good and best practice.

5. You can buy success by throwing money at a challenge, but so can others. There is no competitive advantage in copying what everyone else is doing. Instead focus on what makes your service or product unique and optimise that for all its worth. Everything else will eventually make you very average.

TIPS ON SELECTING CHANGE INITIATIVES

Strategic Change implies that it's Change you can plan and prepare for, like software upgrades, relocations, mergers, new technology and many other things that you can see coming.

With proper resourcing, a clear definition of success and a timely start there really is no reason why strategic Change should fail as often as it does.

Here are some tips on how to select the most effective Change initiatives and avoid failure:

1. Probably not what you want to hear right now, but if it sounds hard and unpleasant, you should probably do that first. On the upside, after those hard miles, everything else will feel easy and pleasant by comparison.

2. If it solves a problem that annoys a lot of people, making that Change a priority will boost morale and create a continuous improvement mindset more than anything else. You can even offer the person who raised the issue to be part of the solution implementation team it that's of interest to them.

3. A Culture Change is never a good place to start. It's much easier to change a culture by making many small adjustments with relatable ideas and changes on things people care about than going all "BIG BANG" about it.

4. There has to be a direct and easy-to-explain link between the Change initiative and customer value. If you can't find it or really struggle to make the connection, it's probably not worth doing. Sorry!

5. Anything to do with upskilling your workforce is the right choice to make. Yes, some will leave and yes some will not be as great as hoped, but what if you don't invest in their development and they all stay?!

TIPS ON OFFERING USEFUL TRAINING

Getting the training plan right is a challenge at the best of times and adding simultaneous Change initiatives to the mix doesn't make it any easier.

While Change is more than just training and comms, training is an important part of building confidence and competence for interacting with the new way of doing things.

Here are some tips on how to offer training that people will appreciate:

1. Create a strategic training plan with a budget, schedule, metrics and clear outcomes to keep things on track and ensure people are trained on time and for the right things.

2. Develop the training material based on a Learning Needs Analysis and create individualised learning plans. After that it's a simple matter of adjusting the materials based on feedback and sharing the final version after the training is done.

3. Involve the most respected subject matter experts in the content design and delivery to give the training that extra layer of credibility it gets from seeing familiar names and faces.

4. Run a few test rounds to be sure that it's as short as possible and practical above all else.

5. Let the executive work through it first. Worst case, they learn something. Best case, they set an example and showcase how important it is to learn these new skills.

6. Offer multi-modal content (video/text/voice), that is engaging, interesting, interactive and makes learners think for themselves. Extra points if you can also offer the option of learning-by-doing in a safe test-environment!

7. Consider a micro learning app to deliver training. A series of daily 10-minute reading tasks and quizzes over a 2-month period (6-8 hours) will be more effective than one big chunk of learning that's never repeated.

8. If you were hoping to use these sessions for some company propaganda or compliance and inclusion theatre, maybe send an email instead and save everyone some time.

STRATEGY #4
SQUEEZING FOR EFFICIENCIES
STARRING MANDY THE MANAGER

HEY GILBURT, I NEED SOME STRATEGIES TO MAKE MY TEAM MORE PRODUCTIVE – ANY IDEAS?

ARE YOU THINKING ADDING RESOURCES, NEW TECH OR PROCESS CHANGES?

I THINK NEW TECH AND PROCESS CHANGES SOUNDS GOOD!

GOTCHA! LET ME DO A BIT OF RESEARCH AND I'LL GET BACK TO YOU.

AH-HA! ANKLE MONITORS, LOCKED DOORS AND NO BREAKS! THANKS GILBERT, YOU'RE A BALL OF INSPIRATION!

WAIT MANDY! YOU CAN'T GO ALL 1984 ON YOUR STAFF!!

TIPS ON SETTING REALISTIC EXPECTATIONS

Change managers are often their own worst enemy when it comes to setting and meeting expectations.

We want the best for people, do a good job and don't mind a serious challenge.

We also don't like saying no, even when we know we should and our better judgment tells us to walk away from what is clearly a Bad Change waiting to happen.

Here are some tips on how to set realistic expectations:

1. Clearly defined success measures are an essential ingredient for Change and a safe haven in times of conflicting opinions and priorities. Don't be the Change superhero who will figure it all out. If success isn't clearly defined, do that first and get everyone to sign off before you start.

2. Call out magical thinking by asking for details on how person X thinks their suggestion could work. You might be considered 'difficult', but keep in mind who will be left to pick up the pieces. That's right, it won't be them doing the work, it'll be you!

3. If you have conflicting priorities due to a lack of resources or different opinions, have a conversation with your sponsor to reconfirm objectives and success measures that were already agreed. Present a clear case on what you need, how it will help and what the consequences to delivery will be to change direction now.

4. Calculate how many hours a task will likely take and match that up to the allocated time. If it doesn't line up you have two realistic options; add more resources or accept a delay.

5. If you are told to do more with less and faster, start looking for an exit. These kinds of Change projects are a burnout waiting to happen and no job is worth your physical and mental health.

STRATEGY #5
HIRING CONSULTANTS FOR EVERYTHING
STARRING STEVE THE SPONSOR

TIPS ON HIRING EXTERNAL EXPERTISE

Consultants, or external experts, have an unfavorable reputation in business land.

Too expensive, only interested in quick wins, too generalist to be useful and out the door before the ink on their glossy reports has even dried, are some of the things said about them. You should always offer the opportunity to solve an issue to your own employees first.

Here are some situations when it's actually better to hire external expertise:

1. It's quite possible that your next Strategic Change challenge depends on skills that you simply don't have in the organisation. A carefully selected consultant with a clearly defined task and suitable skillset is exactly what you need then.

2. Even if you have the skills and expertise, you might not have enough of both to get the Change done within the project timeframe. Adding some external expertise and capacity to your Change team will give them the boost and reach to get the job done on time without losing sleep or having to cut corners in service delivery and product development.

3. Every consultant accepts the risk that they get blamed when things go wrong, it comes with the job and considerable paycheck. You'll want to carefully consider if you'd like to involve your permanent employees in a project with a high risk of failure and stress or let an 'outsider' carry the risk of that first attempt while your staff stand by and learn from the experience.

4. Sometimes Change projects involve a specific task that only needs to be done once. Training staff and backfilling positions to perform that one-off task with no future value to anyone's role isn't always a good option. Let a consultant do it while everyone else focuses on their jobs that keep the business going.

5. No matter how innovative and self-reflecting you are, blind spots and assumptions creep into every process and role eventually. Having a consultant join the Change team for a while can provide a fresh perspective that sparks new ideas, offers different solutions and challenges the status quo everyone else takes for granted by now.

STRATEGY #6
NOT BUDGETING FOR CHANGE ACTIVITIES
STARRING CHRISTINE THE CEO

TIPS ON PLANNING CHANGE

Someone clever once said: "The best time to plant a tree was 20 years ago, the second best time is today". They had a point, especially when it comes to Change strategies.

Coming up with a strategy too late is still better than not having one at all, but it's better to do it at the end of the financial year, right after the annual strategy update or even in the final stage of the Change you are delivering right now!

Here are some tips on what to keep in mind while planning:

1. Find the connection to the strategic plan and make it as obvious as can be. This connection is the first thing people will look for and you want to make it easy for them, so you can spend more time talking about the details.

2. Talking about wonderful possibilities and a bright future is the best fun you can have at work, but someone has to pay for all that goodness. First, get a budget sorted that informs your scope and constraints and what promises you can make.

3. Unless you already have a dedicated Change team (good on you if you do!) it's a smart move to start putting together a Change team as soon as possible. The people and resources you want are probably in high demand so get in there early and secure them while you can.

4. With the right kind of support everyone can be part of a Change team, but Change work is hard work and some projects really take it out of you. Before asking people to sign up for the next gig, check their readiness and fatigue levels and workload. Find a way to give them a break between Change initiatives so they can continue to do their best work.

5. Consider dependencies across the organisation, what else is going on? Sometimes timing is just unfortunate and you'll have to push through. However, often enough a bit of planning and scheduling goes a long way toward not flooding everyone with five big Change initiatives at the same time.

TIPS ON TIME FRAMING CHANGE PHASES

It's often a shock to executives and leaders when they find out how long Change actually takes.

They can't make sense of a timeframe of 6-18 months with neatly organised strategic change activities in project plans, Venn diagrams and Gantt charts. You can almost see the wheels turn and hear them thinking that surely you are exaggerating and that for this Change it will be much quicker than that. Yeah, probably not!

Here are some tips on time framing the Five Phases of Change*:

1. Phase 1 is all about sense making and getting the word out there, expect this to take anywhere between 4-8 weeks to get most people on the same page.

2. Phase 2 is where you assess and negotiate involvement from key stakeholders. Some will be quick to jump on board, others will wait and see and some will decide this is not for them. Either way, you'll know what's what in 6-12 weeks.

3. Phase 3 is for preparation, training, skills building and knowledge transfer. It depends on the type and scope of your Change, but anywhere between 8-24 weeks will cover all but the most complicated Change initiatives.

4. Phase 4 is where all the team's hard work is put into practice. Things will go wrong, problems will need solving and unexpected issues will emerge. More time is better, but anything between 16-24 weeks is a realistic goal.

5. Phase 5 is for evaluation and sustaining the Change in 'business as usual' operations and processes. Allow somewhere between 4-12 weeks, depending on how successful the implementation went and capture as many lessons learned as possible.

If you do the math, your shortest path is 38 weeks (9 months) and the longest path 78 weeks (18 months). A phased overview of activities will clarify why you need this much time to do Change right.

* We chose a 5-phase approach, you can use however many phases you like of course!

TIPS ON HOW TO CHANGE YOUR CULTURE

Culture Change initiatives are the answer when you don't know what else to do. You don't get any points for stating that culture starts with the 'tone at the top', everyone knows that, right?!

Yes, and still we hear too many stories about shameful criminal acts, toxic cultures, excess, greed and leadership behaviours that make you wonder what is wrong with those people…

Here are some tips on how to do Culture Change right:

1. Culture is not a project, it's a multi-year strategic program that requires careful planning, a method or model and dedicated resources, If that's how you feel about it, you're doing it right.

2. Take your time, you'll be here a while. It's been researched time and time again that successful Culture Change takes anywhere from 3 to 7 years, so if you feel it can be done in 6 to 9 months tops, you're wrong.

3. We humans have a weird fixation to focus on what's wrong, leaving people with a sense of inadequacy and underperformance when it's Culture Change time. How about we start celebrating what is good and using that to fix what can be better?

4. By now most of us know that storytelling can be a very powerful tool in Culture Change. Collect and tell stories that share the values of the business at any opportunity, if told well, people will never get tired of it.

5. Fire toxic elements like micromanagers, egomaniacs, bullies and gossips real quick. They can use all that free time to work on themselves and be better humans. Offer support if they are open to that, just don't let the team suffer from someone else's mental health issues.

6. Culture is a shared responsibility. Yes, Change starts at the top, but it works much better when every level joins in decision making, role modelling desired behaviours and fostering a feedback culture. Use the power of many hearts and minds for good!

7. Measure your progress using meaningful metrics and visualisation. These tools will help you tell the story of the culture change and if displayed in an open space will become part of the shared reality of everyone involved.

TIPS ON CHOOSING A PROJECT NAME

Humans are funny in the way we assign names to things to make sense of them.

Without names we'd end up using very long descriptions, flapping our arms a lot or carrying around a book of pictures to explain what we mean.

The importance of naming a change appropriately often gets underestimated and considered trivial until you can practically hear the eye-roll every time you mention project Phoenix, Synergy, Butterfly, New Dawn, Sunrise, Horizon or our personal favourite, Icarus.

Here are some tips on how to choose a good name for your Change:

1. Make it relevant to the Change outcome. If you need a service score of 90% by 2023, Project 90/23 is simple and straightforward enough. Remember, you're going for understanding, not the Pulitzer Prize.

2. If you end up with a long project name, check your acronyms. Unless you're going for cringy or inappropriate innuendos, best avoid things like: the Strengthening Internal Compliance Knowledge Project.

3. Leave the pop culture reference for the Tuesday night trivia at the pub. You might love Star Trek, Star Wars, Brooklyn 99, the Office or Parks and Recreation but your aim is maximum inclusion and understanding, rather than a not-so-subtle nod and wink to the in-crowd.

4. Run a contest with a fun prize and some guidance on what you're looking for and let employees nominate and vote for names. Make sure to have a set of honourable mentions and backup options just in case of a 'Changey McChangeface' situation.

5. Adopt the name staff use for the project in everyday conversation. They often pick the name of a system, process or key component and that's fine, as long as everyone knows what is meant, you might as well go with that.

STRATEGY #10
RUNNING CHANGE LIKE A MILITARY OPERATION
STARRING THE PROJECT CONTROL BOARD

TIPS ON LEADING STRATEGIC CHANGE

Fortunately, most Change initiatives don't involve life-or-death situations. It's more likely they have goals like growth, efficiency, product development or implementing a system or process.

However, using combat-like analogies and language can quickly create a very hostile and counterproductive atmosphere between teams and even influence the organisational culture to a point of 'winning at all cost' with or without a clearly identified 'enemy'.

Here are some tips on leading Change strategically without blowing stuff up:

1. The best fight is the fight you never have, so think, analyse and outsmart the competition using data, customer feedback and innovative ideas.

2. Competitiveness is good, but ethics and values are better. Your employees will mimic your behaviour and you'll want them to always have the moral (and legal) high ground. Set the standard you want to see and lead by example by doing what's right, especially when that's the harder option.

3. Avoid pithy and aspirational one-liners that mask complexity and oversimplify the Change ahead. Instead provide consistent guidance and a realistic vision of what's to come.

4. Hope, denial, doubling down, myopia and arbitrariness are the worst types of 'strategies' and can have very serious and destructive long-term consequences. If that's all you can come up with, get help immediately!

5. Mind your language and focus on your own strengths. No one needs to be defeated or crushed, you're not at war for talent or clients, the business is not actually cut-throat at the frontline. Why so angry?!

6. The only map allowed should be a strategic road map and no, it doesn't need tanks, skulls and minefields. It's okay if it has unicorns.

DOING GOOD

National Homeless Collective

We wanted this book to be more than lots of tips and laughs, so we're donating all the profits to charity. Our hope is that we'll sell many, many copies and get to help even more people!

We believe the National Homeless Collective does incredibly important and much needed work for the most vulnerable people in society and through buying this comic book you're helping to end homelessness, domestic violence and social disadvantage.

You can read all about their nation-wide projects, check out how you could get involved and might even want to make a donation. We know from our own experience they make the most of every dollar they get (https://www.nhcollective.org.au).

THANK YOU FOR READING BAD CHANGE!

WHETHER YOU LOVED IT OR HATED IT,
WE WOULD LOVE TO HEAR FROM YOU!

PLEASE TAG US AND USE
#BADCHANGE ON LINKEDIN

Printed in Great Britain
by Amazon